Deadliest Diseases
of All Time

Polio

Timothy
Grayson-
Jones

Cavendish
Square
New York

Published in 2015 by Cavendish Square Publishing, LLC
243 5th Avenue, Suite 136, New York, NY 10016

Copyright © 2015 by Cavendish Square Publishing, LLC

First Edition

Website: cavendishsq.com

This publication represents the opinions and views of the author based on his or her personal
experience, knowledge, and research. The information in this book serves as a general guide only. The
author and publisher have used their best efforts in preparing this book and disclaim liability rising directly
or indirectly from the use and application of this book.

CPSIA Compliance Information: Batch #WW15CSQ

All websites were available and accurate when this book was sent to press.

Library of Congress Cataloging-in-Publication Data

Grayson-Jones, Timothy.
 Polio / Timothy Grayson-Jones.
    pages cm. — (Deadliest diseases of all time)
 Includes bibliographical references and index.
 ISBN 978-1-50260-088-2 (hardcover) ISBN 978-1-50260-089-9 (ebook)
 1. Poliomyelitis—History—Juvenile literature. 2. Poliomyelitis—Vaccination—History—Juvenile literature.
 I. Title.

 RC180.9.G73 2015
 616.8'35—dc23

2014026350

Editor: Kristen Susienka
Senior Copy Editor: Wendy A. Reynolds
Art Director: Jeffrey Talbot
Senior Designer: Amy Greenan
Senior Production Manager: Jennifer Ryder-Talbot
Production Editor: David McNamara
Photo Researcher: J8 Media

The photographs in this book are used by permission and through the courtesy of: Cover photo and page 1, Science VU/
CDC/Visuals Unlimited/Getty Images, Sajjad Hussain/AFP/Getty Images; Library of Congress/File:Portrait of Sir Walter
Scott-LCCN2002695072.jpg/Wikimedia Commons, 4; Everett Collection/Newscom, 7; Henry Lytton Cobbold/File:Heine
Plus3 WS.jpg/Wikimedia Commons, 8; Jill Freedman/Premium Archive/Getty Images, 13; NYPL/Science Source/Photo
Researchers/Getty Images, 14; Keystone Features/Hulton Archive/Getty Images, 15; Stan Honda/AFP/Getty Images, 16;
Laguna Design/Science Photo Library/Getty Images, 18; Margaret Bourke-White/The Life Picture Collection/Time & Life
Pictures/Getty Images, 21; Ed Clark/The LIFE Images Collection/Getty Images, 23; Peerayot/Shutterstock.com, 27; Everett
Collection/Newscom, 28; Bill Strout/U.S. National Archives and Records Administration/File: EPA Gulf Breeze Laboratory.
Dr. John Couch, Pathobiologist Works At The Electron Microscope. This Is One Of The... - NARA - 546311.jpg/Wikimedia
Commons, 30; Mike_Pellinni/iStock/Thinkstock.com, 33; Nigel Cattlin/Visuals Unlimited/Getty Images, 35; Charles E.
Steinheimer/The LIFE Picture Collection/Getty Images, 37; CDC/Nadya Belins, 39; Alfred Eisenstaedt/Pix Inc./The LIFE
Picture Collection/Getty Images, 40; Hulton Archive/Getty Images, 43; And Deni Mcintyre Will/Getty Images, 47; Farooq
Naeem/AFP/Getty Images, 48; Chris Hondros/Getty Images, 51; Jasper Juinen/Bloomberg/Getty Images, 55.

Printed in the United States of America

Contents

Introduction

Researchers presented a paper in May 2014 about a group of children in California who showed symptoms of a polio-like disease. All five children suffered **paralysis** in at least one of their limbs. All five had been vaccinated against poliomyelitis, also known as the polio **virus**, so they were suffering from a rare, but related, virus. Despite treatment, the five were still struggling with symptoms.

What makes a story like this so frightening is that the eradication of polio with the use of **vaccines** had been a scientific success story. While polio was first documented in 1789 by a British doctor named Michael Underwood, there is anecdotal evidence of the disease dating back throughout early history. In the Carlsberg Museum in Copenhagen, Denmark, there is a carved stone plaque from the time of the New Kingdom Period of Egypt circa 1300 BCE. It shows a man with a withered right leg and a dangling foot. He stands with the help of a cane. It is very likely that the man was a survivor of polio.

Sir Walter Scott, a Scottish author, was one of the first people documented as having a polio-like disease.

One of the first recorded cases of polio is that of Sir Walter Scott, the Scottish author of such adventure books as *Waverley* and *Ivanhoe*. Scott was born in Edinburgh, Scotland, in 1771. As a child, he suffered an attack of fever that lasted for three days. When it ended, he was unable to use his right leg. He had always been active and athletic. He found paralysis unbearable. He struggled against the weakness in his leg and walked long distances outdoors, at first dragging, and then slowly re-strengthening, his leg. In time, he regained his health and was even able to run and jump again.

The word "poliomyelitis" comes from the Greek words *polios*, which means "gray," and *myelos*, which means "matter." The last words, or suffix, "-itis," means "inflammation." Polio strikes the body's central **nervous system** (CNS). If your CNS is damaged, you lose the ability to move or easily control certain muscles, depending on what part of the CNS is affected. Some individuals are left totally unable to move the affected parts of their body—those parts are paralyzed. In others, their limbs become only partially paralyzed, which causes them to shrivel from lack of use and become deformed.

Unlike many diseases, it is often strikingly clear when someone is suffering from polio—children (or former U.S. president Franklin Delano Roosevelt) in wheelchairs, people with smaller, atrophied arms or legs, or worse yet, confined to an **iron lung** in order to help them breathe. For many decades, scientists could do little

Former U.S. president Franklin D. Roosevelt suffered from polio but never let the disease get the better of him.

to treat the disease—they knew its symptoms but had no idea how it was transmitted, or what caused the illness. Luckily, the twentieth century would see significant progress in turning polio from a horrifying disease to one that could possibly be completely eradicated.

one A Crippling Disease

n 1789, Michael Underwood, an English physician, noticed a disease he was seeing more and more frequently, with more cases occurring in the countryside than in the city of London. He provided a clinical description of the symptoms he observed, but the disease itself remained nameless. Within the next fifty years, an increase of outbreaks pushed a German physician by the name of Jacob von Heine to study and provide the first medical report and book on the disease. In his book, he hypothesized that the disease was **contagious** and identified a number of treatment options, including warm baths as well as vigorous exercise. These treatment options were used for more than a century and a half.

In 1887, a Swedish doctor named Karl Oskar Medin realized that there were different forms of the

(From left to right) Jakob von Heine, Karl Oskar Medin, and Ivar Wickman statues at Warm Springs, once a recovery spa for polio sufferers.

disease. He recognized that the onset of the symptoms was made up of two fevers. The first fever was simply a fever, while the second attacked and damaged the central nervous system.

The first recorded polio **epidemic** in the United States was in 1894, when 132 cases occurred in Vermont. In 1904, Austrian physicians Karl Landsteiner and Erwin Popper identified the disease as a virus and named it poliovirus; however, throughout the nineteenth century it was most commonly known as "infantile paralysis." In 1905, a Swedish pediatrician named Ivar Wickman dealt with an outbreak of more than 1,000 cases of the disease. He named it the Heine-Medin disease. In 1907, he investigated whether the disease was indeed contagious, as Heine had believed. If it was contagious, he wanted to know how it spread. He wanted to find out whether children got sick only from direct contact with children who were already sick, or whether they could get sick from **carriers**—people who are infected but do not get sick or show signs of the disease. Carriers are dangerous because they unknowingly carry and spread disease to people who will get sick and suffer harmful symptoms. If people could be carriers of polio, Wickman reasoned, that would explain how it could spread so quickly and so fatally despite keeping the sick separated from healthy people. Wickman thought that many, many people were carriers.

Polio Strikes New York City

In the summer of 1916, a terrible outbreak of polio dominated New York City. Doctors diagnosed 9,000 cases. More than 2,300 people died. The people of New York were terrified. The outbreak started in an Italian neighborhood in Brooklyn. People immediately blamed the immigrants. The city government contacted the officials at Ellis Island, but they knew nothing. No immigrants had entered the United States who were already sick with polio. The officials at Ellis Island then contacted the Italian government to see if there had been any polio outbreaks in the towns and cities from which the immigrants had come, but there was no answer to be found there either.

At that time, doctors still did not know how polio travels from one person to another, but they did know that many diseases live in dirt and garbage. The mayor ordered the streets of New York to be kept clean and that all garbage be disposed of properly and quickly. Realizing that quarantining, or secluding, people had worked in the past to stop the spread of diseases, he forced the sick people into **quarantine**, either at home or in the hospital.

The quarantine regulations were incredibly strict. Parents who could not fulfill them at home had to send their children to the hospital; people who did not have enough space or money to create perfectly clean hospital conditions in a separate room in their home could not keep their children. The idea of sending a child to a polio ward full of sick children and strange nurses and doctors was terrifying. It was even scarier than trying to nurse a paralyzed child at home with no medicine and no experience. Some parents were so afraid to let their children go away that they hid them. If a family refused to send a sick child to the polio ward, the mayor sent police officers to take the child by force.

Trying to Find Patterns

The authorities were desperate to understand the disease so they could be certain that the restrictions they were enforcing were actually the right way to control it. They searched tirelessly for patterns. At one point, in July, they became convinced that African American children did not get polio. In fact, as a weird extension of this idea, they suggested it was also possible that blond children caught it more easily than dark-haired children. However, by August, the hospital wards were full of all types of children and it was clear that there was no difference in susceptibility between black children and white children—or among blonds, brunettes, or redheads.

Some people believed that the disease was carried by cats and dogs. Certain infectious diseases, such as rabies, are carried by animals and are deadly to human beings. Desperate to try any solution, the people of New York started to kill every animal they could find.

During the 1916 polio epidemic, thousands of cats were killed, suspected of being carriers of the disease.

They captured and put to sleep both stray animals and their own pets. By the middle of July, people were killing between 300 and 400 animals a day. At the end of July, *The New York Times* announced that roughly 72,000 cats had died in the war on polio.

Rethinking the Spread of Polio

As New York City got cleaner and cleaner, doctors started to recognize that polio appeared no matter how clean a place was. It attacked every area of the city. It struck rich people and poor people, tidy people and messy people.

Early in August 1916, a comparison between the spread of polio on two New York City islands

A Closer History

1771 In Edinburgh, Scotland, the first case of the disease later identified as polio is reported.

1789 English doctor Michael Underwood recognizes and describes the still unnamed disease.

1887 Swedish doctor Karl Oskar Medin further defines the disease.

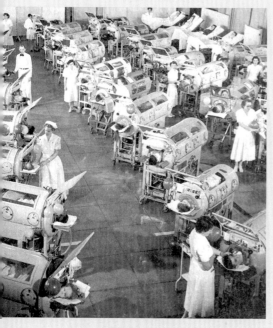

A hospital room full of polio patients in iron lungs.

1916 Polio epidemic breaks out in New York City. Doctors diagnose 9,000 cases and more than 2,300 people die.

1926 Franklin Delano Roosevelt turns Warm Springs into a rehabilitation center for polio patients.

1940 Sister Elizabeth Kenny moves to the United States to treat polio patients.

1941 National Foundation for Infantile Paralysis (NFIP) officially endorses Kenny's methods to treat polio patients.

Dr. Jonas Salk

1951 Basil O'Connor hires Jonas Salk (at left) to create a dead-virus polio vaccine.

1952 Salk tests the newly developed vaccine at D. T. Watson Home for Crippled Children.

1954 Salk's polio vaccine tested on almost two million children. This was the largest medical experiment in history.

1962 Albert Sabin's live-virus Oral Polio Vaccine (OPV) is officially accepted by doctors.

1999 Only 5,000 cases of polio are reported worldwide as a result of rigorous efforts to vaccinate as many people as possible.

2013 According to the Centers for Disease Control and Prevention (CDC), 416 cases are reported worldwide, mainly in African and Middle Eastern nations.

2014 India and ten other nations in Southeast Asia are certified polio-free by the CDC, who estimates that 80 percent of the world's population lives in polio-free regions.

Residents on Governor's Island in the New York City did not contract polio.

demonstrated that dirt might have nothing to do with the spread of polio. Barren Island in Jamaica Bay, Brooklyn, was one of the dirtiest places in New York. Barren Island was where the garbage barges took all of the garbage from every neighborhood in New York City. There were countless rats on Barren Island, as well as flies, cockroaches, and mosquitoes. There was no public water system, no sewage system, and no garbage collection. *There were also no cases of polio.* There were 350 children younger than sixteen years of age on Barren Island and not a single one of them had the disease.

The other island was Governor's Island, which the military owned. There was no polio among the 100 children on Governor's Island either. A doctor in New York noticed this. He believed the lack of polio on both islands was due to isolation. The one thing the islands had in common was that the people living on them were separated from the people and the living conditions in the rest of New York. These people did not come into contact with infected people or objects infected people had touched, and therefore they did not catch the disease.

Lessons from the 1916 Outbreak

The 1916 New York epidemic helped scientists and public health officials understand polio. They finally understood that the disease was contagious, but animals were not carriers. However, people could carry the disease without showing any symptoms. They spread the disease without knowing they were infecting their friends and family.

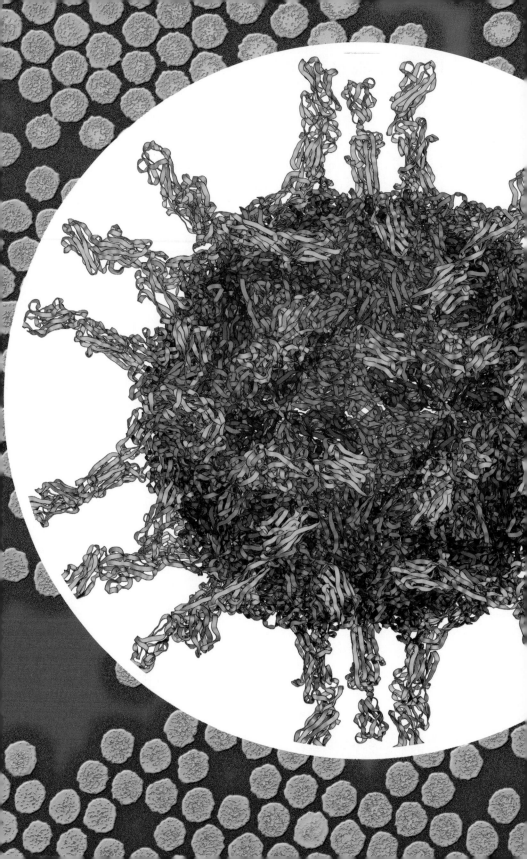

two Unlocking the Secrets of Polio

Cases of polio have been recorded as early as Egyptian times, but epidemics of the disease were far more prevalent in the twentieth century. Diseases that increase in frequency as conditions improve are called "diseases of development." Improvement in sanitation protects people from exposure to germs. However, limited exposure to germs can build **immunity** to some diseases. This is why the Europeans who colonized America did not die from the diseases they'd brought with them, while these same diseases killed the Native Americans who had no previous exposure to them. Polio is the same—repeated exposure to the disease can help the body build immunity to the disease.

Before modern times, conditions were much more **unsanitary**. Almost every child came into contact with poliovirus as an infant. In very tiny children, polio **infection** is usually mild, or **asymptomatic**.

An artist's representation of the human poliovirus.

Children may have the virus in their bodies, but often they do not get sick. However, someone who encounters polio for the first time as an older child or adult is more likely to experience severe effects like paralysis or death.

At the end of the nineteenth century, most people in major cities in Europe and the United States had indoor plumbing. When indoor plumbing became common, most people were not exposed to poliovirus until they were older and more vulnerable to the harmful effects of the disease. They would often come into contact with the virus at school, where they encountered and played with other children who were infected, or by going swimming in a public pool in which infected people had swum.

The President Who Suffered from Polio

Perhaps the most famous victim of polio is Franklin Delano Roosevelt, who served as the United States president from 1933 to 1945. In 1921, when he was thirty-nine years old, he contracted the disease. Although tragic for Roosevelt personally, the disease did find a tough opponent in the future president. He was wealthy, powerful, and determined to put an end to the disease. He declared a war on polio and established the National Foundation for Infantile Paralysis (NFIP). The NFIP declared it would not rest until it found a cure.

Roosevelt was paralyzed from the waist down after having suffered a fever for three days. Nevertheless, he was an athlete and a fighter. He refused to believe his paralysis was permanent. He was determined to regain the use of his legs. He found a spa in Georgia called Warm Springs, a place where people went to recover from various illnesses. He traveled there to see if bathing in the springs would help him.

Warm Springs

Polio patients with physiotherapists at Warm Springs.

Warm Springs is a group of mineral springs that is naturally heated by the Earth to eighty or ninety degrees. Hot mineral baths are often prescribed for people with muscular pain. They help increase blood flow to the muscles and relieve pain due to lack of movement. Bathing at Warm Springs was ideal for a polio patient who had developed poor circulation and had trouble moving.

Roosevelt thought Warm Springs was a miracle for polio patients. In 1926, he decided to buy Warm Springs and turn it into a center for the rehabilitation of polio patients. He wanted it to be staffed by **physiotherapists**, people who are trained in physical therapy. They would work with the patients in the pool, guiding them in exercises designed to rebuild their strength.

At this time, Roosevelt had a business partner, a lawyer named Basil O'Connor. When Roosevelt was elected governor of New York in 1928, he handed over the management of Warm Springs to O'Connor, who ran the spa with a savvy business sense and with passion. The fight against polio was also his fight. Not only was Roosevelt, who was one of his best friends, a victim, so was his youngest daughter. Although his primary concern was to find a cure, O'Connor knew that, in the meantime, he needed to find an effective treatment to ease the pain of polio. Eventually he did, from an unexpected and controversial source—a woman named Elizabeth Kenny.

New Treatment Methods

Since scientists who worked in the early part of the twentieth century had no real understanding of how polio works inside the body, doctors were unsure how to treat it. Most followed a method suggested by Heine, who believed that paralyzed arms and legs should be immobilized. They used splints to force patients' limbs to stay straight. These splints were metal bars that were secured to the sides of a patient's legs with leather straps.

Not everyone agreed that this was the best way to treat paralysis. One person who disagreed was an Australian woman named Elizabeth Kenny. Kenny was born in 1880 and grew up on farms in New South Wales and

Sister Elizabeth Kenny changed the way for which some polio patients were cared.

Queensland. She became interested in medicine after breaking her wrist in a riding accident as a teenager. She first tested her medical knowledge on her younger brother, Bill. She was convinced that his growth from a skinny boy into a vigorous man was the result of the exercises she made him do. Kenny trained as a nurse and worked in the Australian outback, fixing broken bones and delivering babies.

In 1911, Kenny was called to a farm to nurse a two-year-old girl crippled with polio. She had never seen anything as awful as the disease that little girl had. There was no known cure, nor was there any real treatment to ease the pain of the paralysis that many polio victims suffered. Kenny had to figure out what to do. The first thing she noticed was that the girl's muscles were wasting away. She wrapped the girl's limbs in hot, wet rags—which later became known as Kenny's hot packs—and moved them to help rebuild the muscles the girl could not use herself. She believed the child's muscles had forgotten how to work and needed to relearn normal movement. When twenty more children in the area came down with polio, Kenny treated six, all of whom recovered.

Kenny served as a nurse in World War I. The soldiers called her Sister Kenny because she was a nurse—not for religious reasons. Sister Kenny discovered that she had a gift for nursing under crisis conditions. After the war, she returned to the Australian outback but did not treat another polio patient until the 1930s. At this time in Australia, doctors like Jean Macnamara were defining the "real" medical treatment for polio. This treatment included immobilization. Kenny thought Macnamara's belief in immobilization was a terrible mistake. She believed that because the splinted limb could not move easily, the muscles would disintegrate even more. Most doctors were more inclined to listen to Macnamara, who was a doctor, than to Sister Kenny, who was "only" a nurse and had no training in orthopedic medicine—the area of medicine that deals with bones and muscles. Then, during a polio epidemic in Melbourne, Kenny treated several severe cases, using her methods with great success. Two orthopedic surgeons took note of her work. Kenny gained a reputation for helping people whom doctors considered hopeless. Despite these successes, people still mistrusted Kenny's methods of treatment.

Kenny's supporters thought she should take her ideas abroad. In 1940, at fifty-nine years old, the Australian health ministry sent Kenny to the United States.

When Kenny arrived in the United States, many American doctors were following Dr. Macnamara's strategy of immobilization. They used splints as a **brace** for limbs, or wrapped them in plaster casts. They were convinced that the sooner the limb was braced, the less likely it was to become twisted or deformed. Kenny feared she would find the same resistance in America that she had in Australia. At that time, there were a lot of polio cases in Minnesota. Kenny traveled to a hospital there and started working with patients and getting positive results. Doctors continued to criticize Kenny's lack of medical background, but parents of polio victims loved her, including Basil O'Connor. He publicly supported Sister Elizabeth Kenny, and in December 1941, the NFIP officially endorsed her treatment methods and published a booklet describing her work. O'Connor—who had by then moved into the positions of chairman of the NFIP, treasurer of Warm Springs, and head of the American Red Cross—wrote the preface.

Sister Kenny had great faith in the strength and self-sufficiency of the patient. She believed there was no need to use the cumbersome equipment on which so many doctors relied. She believed in reeducating patients and their muscles to stand and walk and run on their own.

Unfortunately, Kenny's muscle theories could not solve all of the problems of polio. One piece of equipment that American doctors used, and that Kenny loathed, was the iron lung. In the same way that she objected to braces, Kenny objected to the machine. She saw it as an external solution that did the work for the patient, allowing them to become weaker and more reliant on machines. She believed the patient needed to do the work alone. She believed only active recovery could restore full health. Sometimes Kenny removed patients from their iron lungs and, using hot packs and massages, helped them breathe again for themselves. However, there were other patients that even Kenny had to admit would die without their iron lungs.

Unfortunately, Kenny's work—though tremendously important to so many sufferers—was only a treatment, not a cure, and it didn't work for everyone. There were many people who were still left crippled or dead. The disease was still in need of a cure.

A Global Search for a Cure

By 1941, Franklin Roosevelt was president of the United States. World War II had begun, and Roosevelt had other issues to concentrate on. It was up to Basil O'Connor to take over the front line of attack in the war on polio. As a result of Roosevelt's diminished efforts, polio research lagged during the war. Then, in 1943, several British and American soldiers in Egypt came down with polio. The Egyptians had believed that

Preventing Diseases with Vaccines

For at least 2,000 years, people have known that someone who recovers from certain infectious diseases will not get sick from them a second time. This is the primary idea behind a vaccine. A vaccine is a little bit of a disease given to a person by a doctor. The person gets infected to a small degree, which raises the level of **antibodies**—the body's defense against disease—and once those antibodies have been produced, the person becomes immune to that disease. In order to make a vaccine safe so that the patient will not actually contract the disease caused by the virus, the doctor weakens or kills the virus before injecting it. Even the weakened or dead virus is enough to help people raise their level of antibodies high enough to ensure immunity to the disease.

President Franklin D. Roosevelt (left) and Basil O'Connor (right).

their country was polio-free before this outbreak. They suggested that the foreigners had brought the disease with them. In fact, there was polio in Egypt, and had been for thousands of years. The difference was that, unlike in America or England, it was usually not fatal. Polio in Egypt tended to end in lameness or a withered arm rather than in severe paralysis or death.

Western doctors noticed that polio in the Philippines, in India, and in Malta behaved similarly to polio in Egypt. At this point, researchers began to see the connection between cleanliness and polio. They realized that people who lived in cities and countries without indoor plumbing or organized trash removal were less likely to get sick from polio than people from England and the United States, where indoor plumbing and greater sanitation were more common.

With this discovery made, O'Connor assumed that the research might progress more quickly. He started looking for scientists who could lead the search for an answer. He found an anatomy professor named Dr. Harry Weaver. Weaver was smart, aggressive, and interested in working with O'Connor. O'Connor made him director of research.

Weaver studied all of the research that had been done on polio. He came to a surprising and dramatic conclusion. He told O'Connor that he believed the only cure for polio was prevention. He said that people had to be stopped from getting the disease at all. Once it took hold of a person, there was no treatment that guaranteed full recovery. Polio patients could never fully undo their paralysis or fully regain the strength and use of their limbs. Weaver believed the only option was to invent a vaccine.

If there are multiple types or strains of a disease, a vaccine will only be effective if it inoculates people from all versions of the disease. Dr. Weaver understood that all versions of poliovirus had to be identified and included in any potential vaccine. Weaver informed O'Connor that the scientists working on the solution would need to work their way through all samples of the poliovirus in order to ensure that all strains were identified and catalogued. With millions of samples to test, the work would be arduous and time-consuming, but any mistakes would make the vaccine ineffective in preventing polio. Weaver had to find a scientist willing to spend perhaps years getting the vaccine ready. One scientist Weaver identified was Dr. Jonas Salk.

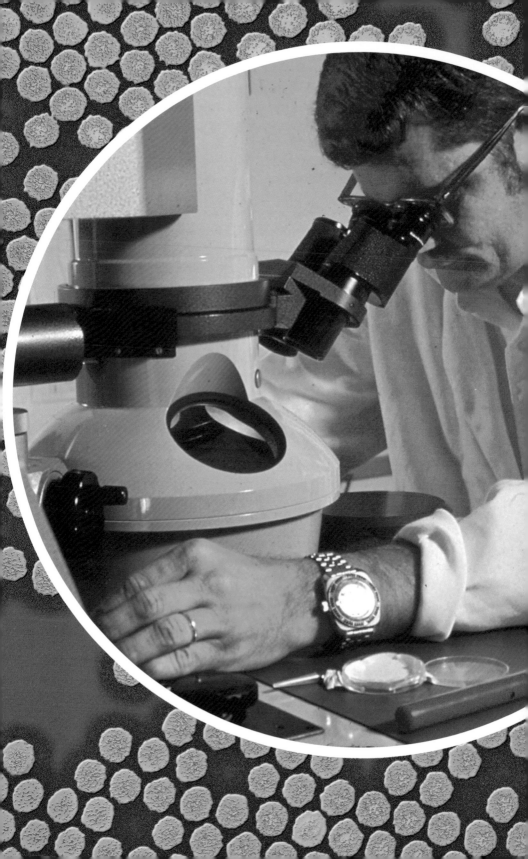

three

Understanding the Science of Polio

As physicians and scientists continued to learn more about polio, they discovered that the ideas Ivar Wickman had were correct. Polio was a contagious disease, but they now needed to know whether polio was caused by a **bacteria** or a virus.

During the first half of the twentieth century, scientists were still attempting to categorize differences between the two, with size being the easiest way to tell the difference—they could see bacteria with a microscope, but the earliest microscopes were not powerful enough to see viruses. Only the invention of the electron microscope would give medical researchers the ability to see things as small as viruses.

The Biological Cause of Polio

Back in the early days of polio research, scientists could determine the presence of a virus only by

Today, scientists are trying to better understand how the poliovirus can be eliminated from Earth completely.

seeing a person or a lab animal become sick from it. In 1908, two scientists in Vienna, Karl Landsteiner and Erwin Popper—the same men who had identified poliovirus in 1904—took fluid from the spine of a polio victim. They put the fluid through a porcelain strainer. The holes in the porcelain were so tiny that it was not possible for any bacteria to pass through them. It was possible for a virus to pass through. Then they injected the filtered fluid into two monkeys. Both of the monkeys became sick with polio. This meant that polio had to be a virus. It also meant that polio could be defeated, as smallpox had been defeated, with a vaccine.

Transmitting Polio

Poliovirus travels from one **host**—the person in which the virus is living—to another via water or the surface of objects. It infects people who drink contaminated water or touch contaminated surfaces and then touch their mouth with their hands. Children are at great risk for infection because they tend to be more careless than adults about touching their mouth with dirty hands. Poliovirus enters and passes through the system of an infected person and is therefore present in human waste and in sewage. This makes it a fecal-oral infection. For example, if untreated sewage containing poliovirus enters a water source, a nonimmunized person who drinks the water can get sick.

There are places all over the world—including the United States—where sewage gets into rivers,

Even in fresh water, poliovirus may lurk.

lakes, and streams. For this reason, it is important
never to drink water from an unknown source. Even
in the wilderness, there is always the chance that a
clear, clean-looking stream has been contaminated
by impurities and disease. After a person is infected
with poliovirus, it enters the stomach. From there,
it travels to the intestine. In the intestine, it burrows
into the cells of the gut mucosa, or intestinal lining.
It infects the cells and then **replicates**, or makes copies
of itself. Each time it replicates, it produces thousands
of new virus particles, or virions, that can travel through
the intestine and reach the sewage system to repeat the
process. Often, the virus has no effect on the person it

Differences Between Bacteria and Viruses

Bacteria are tiny organisms that live in the environment, in plants, and in animals, including human beings. Some bacteria are beneficial to humans, others are deadly. Bacterial diseases and infections in humans can often be treated with antibiotic medications such as penicillin: "anti" means against and "biotic" means bacterial. Viral infections often look like bacterial infections, but they cannot be cured by antibiotics or other known medications. At this point, the only known weapon against a virus is vaccination. Viruses are different from bacteria in several important ways. Viruses are much smaller than bacteria and cannot be seen under a regular microscope but only under an electron microscope. They do not reproduce independently, like other organisms, but only copy themselves in the process of infecting another organism's cells, like those in a person. As a result, viruses are not exactly "living" organisms.

In 1935, two years before the discovery of the electron microscope, the first virus was isolated. Called the tobacco mosaic virus, this virus infected plants. Although they could not see the virus, scientists discovered that they could separate it from other material. Scientists isolated a

Light green and brown spots on the tobacco plant signal where the tobacco mosaic virus has affected the plant.

sample of the tobacco virus and stored it for a long time without feeding it. They then put the virus onto a healthy tobacco plant. The plant immediately became sick. This meant that the virus had remained infectious without eating or reproducing. It did not age or change while in storage. This is not the way a living organism behaves.

has infected. Other times it has a minor effect, making the person mildly sick but not dangerously ill. One percent of the time, poliovirus travels from the mucous lining of the intestine into the bloodstream. From here, it can invade the nervous system. It is only if it enters the central nervous system that polio can cause paralysis.

Poliovirus operates on a microscopic level. When scientists say that it burrows into the intestinal lining, this means that a particle of poliovirus attaches itself to a single cell of the intestinal lining. The human body is made up of millions and millions of cells. A cell is so tiny that it can be viewed only under a microscope. Each cell in the human body has a nucleus in its center, which is the "brain" of the cell; a cell wall, which lets food into the cell and waste out of the cell; and proteins. When a particle of poliovirus reaches a cell, it attaches itself to a specific protein on the surface of the cell called a poliovirus receptor (PVR). The PVR creates a bridge between the inside and the outside of the cell. Poliovirus attaches to the PVR on the outside of the cell and then, when the PVR moves back inside the cell, the poliovirus tries to go in with it. This is a common strategy for a virus because it needs to get into the cell in order to replicate.

Viruses such as polio are dangerous to cells because they destroy a cell's ability to function properly. Instead of doing its job maintaining the health of the body, the cell is taken over and turned into a virus factory. When the virus has replicated as much as it can in that cell, it shuts down the cell's own processes and waits for the cell to die. Then the cell dies or bursts in a process called lysis. The bursting releases all the new pieces of virus into the body. They find new healthy cells to infect, attaching to their PVR particles and widening the circle of infection.

Continuing to Study Polio

Despite the fact that polio has now been successfully conquered by a vaccine, scientists still do not completely understand how the virus spreads through

Mice and rats used in poliovirus experiments at Stanford University in California.

the body. Some researchers think the virus travels through the bloodstream. Others think it is able to go directly to the nerves. In one experiment, scientists bred mice to be genetically susceptible to polio. This meant that every mouse would get sick. They injected each mouse in the left leg with poliovirus. The virus moved from the left leg to the spinal cord to replicate. Interestingly, even though the spinal cord is in the middle of the body, the left leg was still the first place to be paralyzed. The scientists then cut the nerves between the left leg and the spinal cord of some mice before they injected the virus. In these mice, the virus did not reach the spinal cord, even though there was still blood moving between the left leg and the spinal cord. This suggests that the virus travels through the nerves to reach the spinal cord and not through the blood. This is only a possibility, however. The fact that this is what happened in genetically engineered mice does not mean it is how a normal infection of polio works in a human being.

Research into polio continues today. Many organizations around the world are working together to learn more about the virus so that they can eliminate it from the planet. Groups such as the World Health Organization (WHO), the United States Centers for Disease Control and Prevention (CDC), Rotary International, and the United Nations Children's Fund (UNICEF) have come together to form the Global Polio Eradication Initiative. This is a group

Members of the Global
Polio Eradication
Initiative committee.

that seeks a polio-free world. To try to combat the
disease, the organization has created a committee that
spearheads and coordinates all global research on polio,
combining the efforts of virologists, epidemiologists,
physicians, sociologists, and public health officials
from many countries around the globe.

four Creating a Polio Vaccine

The creator of the polio vaccine, Dr. Jonas Salk, was born in New York City in 1914, two years before the infamous polio outbreak that struck the city in 1916. Salk was only fifteen years old when he entered college, studying at City College in New York. Afterward, he attended New York University School of Medicine. It did not take long for Salk to discover his area of specialty, immunology. His two lectures in medical school were about immunizing people with a **toxin** and the concept that exposure to a disease can help people build immunity to the disease.

After New York University, Salk went to the University of Michigan, where he worked with Dr. Thomas Francis, who was developing a vaccine for influenza using dead, or inactivated, viruses. From Michigan, Salk went to Pennsylvania, where he began to pursue his own work. When Dr. Harry Weaver called him to help with the polio project, Salk was very interested. Most of the people involved in polio work

Dr. Jonas Salk was a key player in developing a polio vaccine.

believed they needed to find a live-virus vaccine, in which a small amount of weakened or altered virus was used. However, influenced by his work with Dr. Francis, Salk believed it might be possible to create a dead-virus vaccine for polio.

In September 1951, the NFIP organized the Second International Poliomyelitis Conference, which Salk attended with Basil O'Connor. Many of the scientists O'Connor had met were interested only in what they did in the lab, but Salk was interested in how science could help people. He became partners with O'Connor, who wanted to find a cure for polio.

In 1952, there were 58,000 new polio cases in the United States. Five thousand people died. Parents kept their children out of school, and avoided movie theaters and beaches. As scary as all this was, the end was in sight. Weaver's scientists now knew that there were only three types of poliovirus, and they knew how to grow them to create a vaccine. They had tested a vaccine that worked on monkeys. The last step was to make one that worked for people.

In the spring of 1952, Salk got permission from the medical director of the D. T. Watson Home for Crippled Children to do a test on the polio patients there. He would inject them with vaccines made of the version of poliovirus they already had. If it raised their antibody levels, he would know the vaccine was working. There was no danger for the patients, because they were already

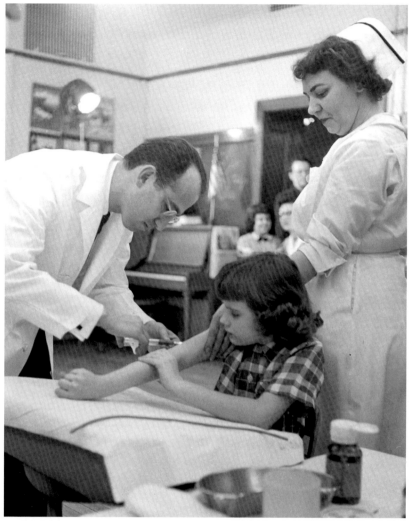

Dr. Jonas Salk vaccinates a young girl with the polio virus.

infected and would not get sicker. When Salk injected
the patients, their antibody levels rose more than they
had when the patients had actually contracted the
disease. Salk then did a second test. He used the vaccine

on a group from the Polk State School, none of whom had ever had polio. This time, the antibody levels rose in people who had never had the disease. Salk's vaccine was a success. The war on polio was nearly won.

One further trial was needed. O'Connor organized the NFIP to test the vaccine on two million children. Some would receive the vaccine, and some would receive **placebos**. The placebo group would think that they were receiving the vaccine, but in reality they would not. This would ensure that any difference in antibody levels between the two groups would be due only to the vaccine and not to the excitement of the trial or some other factor the scientists had not taken into consideration. Every major scientific trial uses a placebo on a control group for this reason. This vaccination project was an enormous undertaking. Tens of thousands of volunteers at NFIP offices all over the country helped organize the vaccine injections.

Although the trial had been risky—nine million dollars had been spent on 27 million doses of vaccine before results were in—O'Connor never questioned that the vaccine would work. His only priority was to make sure that as many children were protected from this awful disease as possible. He bought the vaccine beforehand because he could think of no worse situation than to have a successful trial and not have paid for enough to protect all the children who wanted the vaccine.

Dead Versus Live

The debate about whether to use live microbes or dead specimens to create a vaccine was not limited to polio, and it is a debate that continues to this day. Many scientists and researchers believe that taking a live virus and diluting its potency is the best way to "teach" the human body's immune system to fight a disease. Measles, mumps, chicken pox, and other childhood illnesses are often combatted with live vaccines. However, live specimens have a few drawbacks—a living microbe could still mutate, becoming more powerful and infect the patient. In addition, live vaccines must be kept refrigerated to remain potent. While this is not a problem in the United States, it does present a challenge to researchers looking to immunize people in the developing world.

Dead microbes (also known as inactivated vaccines) are easier to store and far less likely to cause the illness they are designed to combat. However, this too has a price, as the immunity built by an inactivated vaccine is far less potent than a live one, resulting in the need for multiple treatments.

The test was a success, and the vaccine was officially pronounced safe, effective, and potent. The American people went crazy. They had waited so long and suffered so much. They adored the quiet, intelligent Dr. Jonas Salk.

The only people who were not excited were other scientists. They objected to the press conferences and magazine pieces that made Salk seem like a movie star. This was not how scientists behaved, they argued. The public assumed that these scientists were just jealous.

However, there were real reasons to take issue with this method of vaccination. The primary objection the scientists had was that Salk's discovery of the polio vaccine was not a discovery at all; it was just an application of ideas that had been around for years. They also argued that the use of the dead-virus vaccine was perhaps not the best answer. It was expensive—three separate injections were necessary. Also, the effects were only temporary—each shot would probably last for no more than a few years, which meant that a booster injection would be needed to revive its strength.

The scientists who made this argument believed that Salk's vaccine was inferior to a live vaccine. A live vaccine would offer permanent immunity. It would also be a scientific advance. There were other scientists who said that criticizing Salk was ridiculous. He had solved a problem that had deeply troubled the world for more than half a century. He had saved millions of lives. In the end, although Salk was adored by the public and was considered a success by most people's standards, he was never recognized as a pioneer by the scientific community.

Using a Live-Virus Vaccine on Polio

Albert Sabin (left), the foremost live-virus vaccine scientist, was very critical of Salk. He, along with many other scientists, thought that Salk had settled for the easy solution. To him, live-virus vaccines were the immunological solutions of the future. Dead-virus vaccines seemed an old fashioned, short-term solution rather than real scientific progress. However, the American public was not interested in what Sabin thought.

Despite the general public's lack of interest in a live vaccine, Sabin continued his research, working overseas. Settling in England, Sabin was able to create a version of the polio vaccine using live viruses. He was able to test this vaccine in 1961, when there was a polio outbreak in Hull, England. The test was a success, and many doctors started using his Oral Polio Vaccine (OPV) the next year.

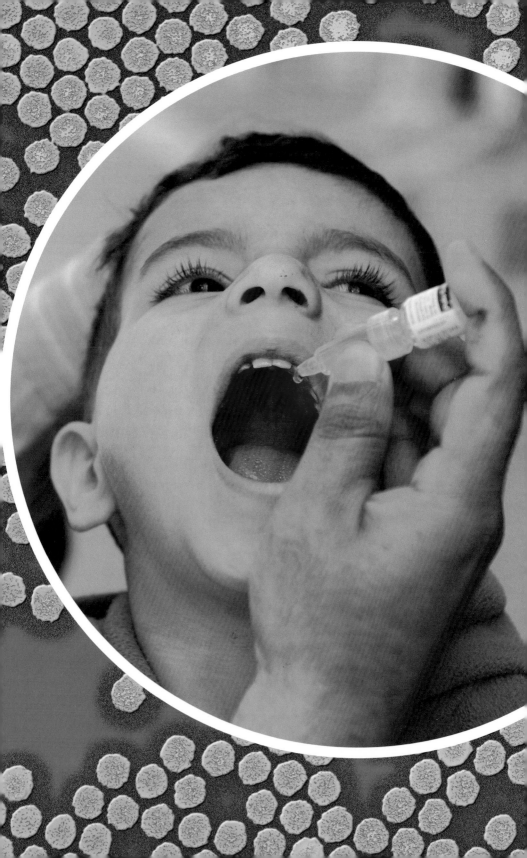

five Continuing the War on Polio

T hanks to the use of both the dead- and live-virus vaccines, scientists have been able to eliminate the risk of polio. There has not been a case of naturally occurring polio in the United States for more than thirty-five years, since a 1979 outbreak among the Amish in the Midwest. The few cases of polio in the 1980s and 1990s came from people traveling abroad or getting the disease from the vaccine itself. To avoid this latter issue, the live vaccine has not been used in the United States since 2000.

Both the live-virus and dead-virus vaccines have benefits and both have risks. One major advantage of the live vaccine is that it is taken orally and does not require a trained medical person to administer it, unlike the Salk vaccine, which is an injection. In addition, it is much less expensive, needs to be given only once, and offers lifelong immunity. The disadvantage is that there is a slight (one in a million)

A young boy receives polio vaccination drops.

risk of paralysis. To administer the Salk vaccine, a trained medical person is needed, and the patient may be required to get a booster shot to maintain long-term immunity. However, there is zero risk of paralysis.

In a short time, the vaccines created by Sabin and Salk eradicated polio in most of the developed world. Today, in parts of the world where there is little money for health care, the less expensive Sabin vaccine is used. Because it is so cost effective, many people believe that it is the Sabin vaccine that makes eradication, or total elimination of polio, a real possibility.

Fighting Polio in Africa

Polio epidemics have been most difficult to control in Africa. In many countries there, health care issues are overlooked because of political problems or war. In some cases, the wartime fighting makes it impossible for health workers to enter a country and vaccinate people. Sometimes health workers request a cease-fire, which is a time when armies agree to stop shooting. When a government at war agrees to a cease-fire, health workers are able to go in and vaccinate the people.

In 2014, an outbreak of polio occurred in Cameroon, and the disease spread to Equatorial Guinea, threating all of Central Africa as well. The difficulty in keeping the disease in check is how few children get vaccinated against polio. The World Health Organization works with most countries to ensure

Polio still affects many people today. This child in Nigeria suffers from polio.

that at least 80, if not 90, percent of the population is inoculated against polio, but in Equatorial Guinea, that number is less than 40 percent.

In recent years, there have been only a few small outbreaks of polio in less developed countries. The problem is that the use of Sabin's live-virus vaccine means that everyone who is vaccinated is actually producing tiny amounts of live virus. This is because

Dealing With Post-Polio Syndrome

Post-Polio Syndrome (PPS) is a reweakening of the muscles that occurs in people who suffered from a polio attack. About 25 percent of people who had polio will eventually suffer from post-polio syndrome.

Doctors do not yet understand the cause of PPS. They do know that during acute poliomyelitis, many motor nerve cells, which tell muscles what to do, die. The remaining cells need to send out new nerve terminals to command the muscles that have lost their own nerve cells. Based on this information, there are four major theories to explain PPS.

1. Thirty or forty years after suffering from polio, the substitute nerve terminals may stop working.

2. The remaining original motor nerve cells may start dying after decades of working for so many extra muscles.

3. PPS could be an autoimmune problem. This means that the immune system (which is designed to fight off disease) of a PPS sufferer attacks the person's body.

4. Poliovirus may reactivate in the bodies of people with PPS. This seems unlikely because people with PPS are not able to infect others with polio.

The fact that so little is known about PPS makes it difficult to treat. It seems true that people who pushed themselves the hardest to regain their strength are now suffering the most. Doctors usually recommend that sufferers slow down and treat themselves more gently. Unlike the war on polio, the war on PPS is not a fight against a disease; it is a battle for the continuing health and comfort of every polio survivor. To learn more about PPS, visit the National Institute of Health's webpage devoted to the topic: www.ninds.nih.gov/disorders/post_polio/detail_post_polio.htm.

Sabin's vaccine actually is the poliovirus. It combines three mutant strains of polio that have the potential to mutate into a deadly form of the virus. This means there may be dangerous viral material in the sewage systems of such polio-free countries as the United States.

There are samples of live poliovirus all over the world. Everyone who has ever studied polio has used real poliovirus, so there are polio samples in thousands of labs and hospitals. If one of these samples were set loose accidentally—or on purpose—it could start another epidemic.

Using Polio as a Biological Agent

Another danger is biological terrorism. Biological terrorism is when one army or country infects the people they are fighting with a disease. There has been accidental and deliberate biological terrorism throughout history. For instance, when Europeans first arrived in America, they brought smallpox with them. Some transferred the disease on unknowingly. Others, such as Lord Jeffery Amherst, infected the populations through careful planning. Hundreds of thousands of Native Americans died in these terrible epidemics.

Polio is a very durable virus. It can survive for long periods of time in water or soil, without a human host. The scary fact is that we do not know how long the virus can survive. It is possible that in areas where drinking water is recycled, the virus could survive

Poliovirus could be introduced to water systems to harm nonimmune populations.

indefinitely. If enough of the virus was created, people could release it onto an unsuspecting public, causing worldwide panic.

Eradicating Polio

If polio can be eliminated by vaccination, why isn't everyone vaccinated? World vaccination is expensive and labor-intensive. Health organizations want to reach a point at which the disease will be eradicated. Unfortunately, it will be hard to know when to stop vaccinations, or if the virus has actually been eliminated. Since the virus could be active for an indefinite period of time, any new generations that are not vaccinated would be at risk of contracting polio.

Some people believe that it would be best to keep vaccinating indefinitely.

There are valid concerns about whether or not keeping the virus is safe. Polio is a perfect weapon for biological terrorism. It travels through water and food. It is extremely difficult to detect, and it is very contagious. In a city of ten million unvaccinated people, at least 7,000 would die in another polio epidemic. However, this does not necessarily mean people should destroy all the existing poliovirus. It is also possible that if all the poliovirus in the world were destroyed, scientists could create more through the use of genetic technology.

Finishing the Task

As world health officials continue to battle the disease, they are able to narrow the number of countries that see outbreaks of polio. According to the Polio Global Eradication Initiative's website, the disease is now endemic primarily in three nations—Afghanistan, Nigeria, and Pakistan. As long as the virus is still active anywhere, it is a global health threat, as it could be carried back to nations where the disease was thought to be eliminated. If this were to happen, any unvaccinated individuals could become victims in a new outbreak. Even once the disease is eradicated, the initiative's work will not be done, as they will constantly need to monitor the population for any reemergence of the original virus or a new post-vaccine version.

Glossary

antibodies Substances in the body present or produced in response to infection.

asymptomatic Showing no symptoms of a disease with which one is infected.

bacteria Microscopic organisms that live in soil, water, or the live bodies of plants or animals; they can be either helpful or harmful to the body they inhabit.

brace A pair of splints connected by leather straps that fastens at the sides of the leg to support weakened muscles.

carrier A person who does not get sick from a disease but can pass it on to others.

contagious A disease that can be passed from one person to another, or a stage of being infected in which one person can pass a disease to another person.

epidemic An outbreak of a disease that spreads widely and rapidly.

Glossary

host The human or animal in which a virus lives.

immunity The ability to resist a disease.

infection Establishment of a sickness in a living organism.

iron lung A machine that inflates and deflates the lungs of people with paralyzed chest muscles so they are able to breathe.

nervous system The brain, nerves, and spinal cord.

paralysis The complete loss of motion and feeling in a body part.

physiotherapist Someone who treats disease physically, using massage, exercise, water, and heat.

placebo Nonactive medicines that patients believe are real.

quarantine To isolate people with a contagious disease so they cannot spread infection.

replicate To copy or reproduce.

toxin A poisonous substance.

unsanitary Unclean.

vaccine An injection, liquid, or pill that produces immunity to a particular disease.

virus Submicroscopic infectious material that causes disease.

For More Information

Interested in learning more about polio? Check out these websites and organizations.

Websites

Brought to Life – The Iron Lung

www.sciencemuseum.org.uk/broughttolife/themes/treatments/iron_lung.aspx

This interactive website explains how the iron lung was invented and used. It provides interesting facts, stories of people who depended on iron lungs for survival, and a moveable drawing of the iron lung itself.

The History of Polio (Poliomyelitis)

www.historyofvaccines.org/content/articles/history-polio-poliomyelitis

This site breaks down the three types of polioviruses and also has some interesting stats about the 1916 New York outbreak.

Polio Global Eradication Initiative

www.polioeradication.org/Home.aspx

The official website of the multinational partnership looking to end the threat of polio throughout the world, this site has videos, links to publications, constant updates, and more.

Whatever Happened to Polio?

amhistory.si.edu/polio/index.htm

A Smithsonian site that looks at the history of polio. The site includes a timeline, historical photos, what is happening today, and more.

Organizations

In the United States:
Centers for Disease Control (CDC)
1600 Clifton Road
Atlanta, GA 30333
Website: www.cdc.gov

The Pan American Health Organization
Regional Office of the World Health Organization
525 Twenty-third Street NW
Washington, DC 20037
Website: www.paho.org

In Europe:
World Health Organization
Avenue Appia 20
1211 Geneva 27
Switzerland
Website: www.who.int

For Further Reading

Bruno, Richard L. *The Polio Paradox: What You Need to Know*. New York, NY: Grand Central Publishing, 2009.

Carstairs, Andrew. *Polio: The Virus and Its Prevention*. New York, NY: Amazon Digital Services, 2014.

Kehret, Peg. *Small Steps: The Year I Got Polio*. New York, NY: Albert Whitman & Company, 2013.

Oshinsky, David. *Polio: An American Story*. New York, NY: Oxford University Press, 2005.

Rogers, Naomi. *Polio Wars: Sister Kenny and the Golden Age of American Medicine*. New York, NY: Oxford University Press, 2013.

Index

Index